The Velvet Protocol
Julia Rose Lewis
&
Nathan Hyland Walker

Newton-le-Willows

Published in the United Kingdom in 2022
by The Knives Forks And Spoons Press,
51 Pipit Avenue,
Newton-le-Willows,
Merseyside,
WA12 9RG.

ISBN 978-1-912211-90-6

Copyright © Julia Rose Lewis & Nathan Hyland Walker, 2022.

The right of Julia Rose Lewis & Nathan Hyland Walker to be identified as the authors of this work has been asserted by them in accordance with the Copyrights, Designs and Patents Act of 1988. All rights reserved. No part of this publication may be reproduced, stored in a retrieval system, transmitted in any form or by any means, electronic, photocopying, recording or otherwise, without prior permission of the publisher.

Acknowledgements:

An early version of 'Navy Bean Soup / Navelbine' was read and discussed as a part of giving the paper 'What is lost when words are wasted between medicine and poetry?' at Poetry in Expanded Translation II at Bangor University.

An early version of 'Navy Bean Soup / Navelbine' was performed at the 2018 Poem Brut at the Rich Mix.

'Bruschetta / Perjeta' was performed at the 2018 Poem Brut at the Writers Centre Kingston.

Pamenar Magazine published 'Dedication,' 'Diet Pepsi / Pepcid,' and 'Bruschetta / Perjecta.'

Marsh Hawk Review published, 'Training for the Grand National,' 'Saffron Zofran,' and 'Beignets Benadryl.'

an iron fist in a velvet glove

Dedication

There was a woman in the doctor's office, like a grandmother in her kitchen, who could tell you about every chemotherapy drug as though it were a meal she had prepared herself for her family. She would tell you the recipe and tricks known only to those who had used the recipe. She would tell you how she felt after the meal, she would tell you everything she knew if you would listen. This book is dedicated to her wisdom. Like a witch she could conjure poison, like a witch, she could nourish you.

The Velvet Protocol

Pivotal or a Viable Alternative

Elizabeth Taylor played the character Velvet in the film National Velvet adapted from the novel by Enid Bagnold by the same name. The name of the horse changed from piebald to pirate like the name of chemotherapy changed from chemical name to brand name, vinorelbine to Navelbine.

Later in her career, Elizabeth Taylor played Cleopatra in the film by the same name. The CLEOPATRA clinical trial showed that first-line treatment with Perjeta, Herceptin, and Taxotere significantly increased progression-free survival for patients with HER2 positive metastatic breast cancer compared with Herceptin and Taxotere.

In the sequel, International Velvet, the character Sarah Velvet Brown describes the trainer for the British equestrian team to her aunt as a velvet fist in an iron glove. The color of the horse was changed from chestnut to liver chestnut. The HERNATA study compared Taxotere and Navelbine in combination with Herceptin in HER2 positive metastatic breast cancer patients and found no benefits, save that the latter had significantly fewer adverse effects.

VELVET

Perez, E.A., López-Vega, J.M., Petit, T. et al. Safety and efficacy of vinorelbine in combination with pertuzumab and trastuzumab for first-line treatment of patients with HER2-positive locally advanced or metastatic breast cancer: VELVET Cohort 1 final results. Breast Cancer Res 18, 126 (2016). https://doi.org/10.1186/s13058-016-0773-6

CLEOPATRA

Swain SM, Baselga J, Kim SB, et al. Pertuzumab, trastuzumab, and docetaxel in HER2-positive metastatic breast cancer. N Engl J Med. 2015;372(8):724-734. http://doi:10.1056/NEJMoa1413513

HERNATA

Andersson M, Lidbrink E, Bjerre K, et al. Phase III randomized study comparing docetaxel plus trastuzumab with vinorelbine plus trastuzumab as first-line therapy of metastatic or locally advanced human epidermal growth factor receptor 2-positive breast cancer: the HERNATA study. J Clin Oncol. 2011;29(3):264-271. http://doi:10.1200/JCO.2010.30.8213

VELVET: the protocol

Patients received a Perjeta loading dose of 840 mg on day 1 of cycle 1, followed by 420 mg on day 1 of subsequent 3-weekly cycles. Herceptin was administered at a loading dose of 8 mg/kg on day 2 of cycle 1, followed by 6 mg/kg on day 1 or 2 of subsequent 3-weekly cycles. Navelbine was administered at an initial dose of 25 mg/m2 on days 2 and 9 of cycle 1, followed by 30–35 mg/m2 on days 1 and 8 or days 2 and 9 of subsequent 3-weekly cycles. All were administered intravenously and were given until investigator-assessed disease progression or unacceptable toxicity.

This is where the metaphor is tried and exhausted. This slip of a young girl falls from the horse after the race and before she is weighed, she is disqualified.

Julia Rose Lewis & Nathan Hyland Walker

Tailoring the Velvet

This will be a short talk on the difference between a velvet covered helmet and a little black dress.

Training for the Grand National

You will need a horse trailer, a rented stall, a lounge line, and more than you imagined. The aim of preparatory medications is to turn a cancer patient into a horse, because horses can generally not vomit or otherwise regurgitate. See Zofran and Ativan now. In need of suceeding, these medications will include intravenous Pepcid, Solumedrol, Benedryl, and Demerol. Goggles, tall boots, gloves oh my!

Julia Rose Lewis & Nathan Hyland Walker
Training Notes

On the addition of Xgeva, Zometa, or the older bisphosphonates to build up the bones, this will double or triple the length of the cycle depending on whether they are given monthly or every six weeks.

Elizabeth Taylor was cast in her first star role in National Velvet on the strength of her riding skills and her accent. Not her height. Filming was delayed until she had grown tall enough.

The Velvet Schedule

The Velvet Protocol

	premeds	antiemetics	chemo
week 1	Pepcid 40mg IVP Solumedrol 15mg IVP Benedryl 25mg IVP Demerol 12.5mg IV PRN x 1	Ativan 0.5mg IV PRN Zofran 8mg IV	Herceptin 825mg IV Perjeta 420mg IV Navelbine 50mg IV Xgeva 60mg subcut
week 2	Pepcid 40mg IVP Solumedrol 15mg IVP	Zofran 8mg IV	Navelbine 50mg IV
week 3			
week 4	Pepcid 40mg IVP Solumedrol 15mg IVP Benedryl 25mg IVP Demerol 12.5mg IV PRN x 1	Ativan 0.5mg IV PRN Zofran 8mg IV	Herceptin 825mg IV Perjeta 420mg IV Navelbine 50mg IV
week 5	Pepcid 40mg IVP Solumedrol 15mg IVP	Zofran 8mg IV	Navelbine 50mg IV
week 6			

Julia Rose Lewis & Nathan Hyland Walker

Hay

It is not a question of violet rage. Nay rather, it is a question of how much hot water one ought to give a sick horse in winter.

Otherwise known as the dose of Solumedrol can be lowered if the patient does not display sensitivity to Herceptin, Perjeta, and Navelbine. Think of the diabetic patients.

The Kitchen Sink: Week 1

Premeds

Pepcid 40mg IVP
Solumedrol 15mg IVP
Benedryl 25mg IVP
Demerol 12.5mg IV PRN x 1

Julia Rose Lewis & Nathan Hyland Walker

Diet Pepsi
Pepcid

In the same lemon as gasoline,
soon gastrin
and the vagus nerve trigger release
of pepsinogen,
it digests itself today
now born pepsin sinning against the diner.

We hate it.

The mother of chaos is
the grandmother of gas and the road
from vast chasm void,
this obsidian is a glass and charcoal act
in between veins of history
I mean like a grandmother in her kitchen,
we take it.

We take another little piece of her volcanic rock
for relief if heartburn fizzes and dazes still.

People will tell you it leads towards cancer,
and I will laugh,
actually cackle like the witch
because coal or charcoal it is important to note
that gas came from chaos
to denote a principle if occult singing.

We respire it.

Sole Mediterranean Solumedrol

Instead of muddling with gin
never alone,
is sole the vehicle in the middle of dill,
lime, and capers,
see a dozen thin files like flatfish.

If sill and the sandal firmament will
allow the soul
to meddle with them garlic power, cumin, peppercorns,
and salt will become pavement.

Filling a midden of garlic and inexperienced onions,
unsalted, the butter becomes caper berries,
about to shallots,
obsolete leaps to cope as goats
says the nanny goat to the kid
remember generous is as generous does need.

Rough and fresh dill to garnish a foolish person
of the parsley family gives a delightful look,
silly in the sense of innocent luck,
musical chairs, dill leaves.

Eye of the grasshopper cheers!

Julia Rose Lewis & Nathan Hyland Walker

Beignets Benedryl

In begetting,
use sugar reverse beer,
if feeding let alone ten minutes and it will foam.

A little feral besting the eggs, salt,
evaporated milk, and then mix the two measures.

Stir half the flour for the shortening
for the stirring into this meaning before others.

Lightening needs.

Transfer to fat and bowl with towel,
and do not disturb for two hours or here.

From the bed of the problem, roll out tired bodies,
they are fried in the deep sense of tried.

This feral lift off will leave inside the hollow lies
as the beignets are finished
in kind to wooden boats.

After dry draining they are given to satin navigation.

The sugar coat will let the sailboat into the wind
and begging the vigor of history I mean.

Antiemetics

Ativan 0.5mg IV PRN
Zofran 8mg IV

Julia Rose Lewis & Nathan Hyland Walker

Saffron
Zofran

In the dominion nausea,
see saffron crocus sings autumn,
and the crows flower a darker lilac crocus sunlight.

Sun bright, satin knows what needs be done
and watches until it is the fragrant hay.

First style, I see saffron fresh,
I see one-hundred and fifty flowers dried is real life;
I wish in crimson,
I wish the stigma of witches in the distance,
I wish in triplet styles.

I have this wish for red maroon down to yellow dishes;
I wish for colors sargol, pushal, bunch, and konge,
with all this might.

Well make a window,
a week or two, and do as crimson dried and threads
sealed in dreams
and all the stigmas, all the wishes will come true,
will thread through saffron nurses.

The Velvet Protocol

Chemotherapy

Herceptin 825mg IV
Perjeta 420mg IV
Navelbine 50mg IV
Xgeva 60mg subcut

Julia Rose Lewis & Nathan Hyland Walker

Hare, Ceps, and Wine Herceptin

The leading hare,
in quarters read dimerization
here cut into seven or eight and brined daytime.

Perception stirs at flour, pepper,
and further salt tossing the hare to coat
in the earthenware oven,
clarified butter is fine to warm two pats to brown
the hare in parts to braise its coat.

Raise the hare,
in the season of natural utterance running
fast to praise her interception.

One large carrot sliced into the earthenware,
add two large onions diced, add the third butter
and sauté until golden onions.

Here print the thyme from the leavings
of five or six sprigs and stir into the earthenware
and stir in five cloves of garlic.

Now wine in order, the hare burgundy to return,
to the earth then weathering
until thinking for thirty minutes more
and more before removing to let simmer itself thick.

On the inception of porcini mushrooms,
from stake and pores,
in a separate pan, it is fine to clarify butter to hear
the penny buns to understand
to entirely take the ceps, stalk, and caps inside.

The Velvet Protocol

Perceive the history of the stone noble,
its nitrogen exchange in the white and pine forest
it is known as squirrels bread.

Once upon a time the boulder in the woodland
and now wine in butter reception,
this garnish was always to finish with parsley as the
mutual tomorrow.

Julia Rose Lewis & Nathan Hyland Walker

Bruschetta Perjeta

Bruschetta is bread and
red and bread
and red tomatoes and yellow tomorrows
and orange tomatoes
and green tomorrows
and purple tomatoes looming
in the middle of the Thursday
and through this day which is old.

The bread should be day old
before toasting,
before rubbing with roast garlic,
do not roast the tomatoes
for they are summoning her
to balsamic, to salt, to pepper, tomorrow.

Now throw the tomato
dice into the bowl with seeds up, with skins up,
face up to
macerate to make soft or made soft or soaked,
to soften in olive from oil
from olive for extra virgin olive oil…
the future of oil is leaving here.

So seeds up, sixes up
to fill the bread,
let the tomatoes fall softly
only onto the bread yet,
bruschetta is simple is still experimental,
appetizer a part of a whole protocol, please see
the velvet protocol.

Navy Bean Soup
Navelbine

A penny for your afternoon?

The stones will be picked over
rinsed, drained, and added to water.

A penny for your rabbit
if given the bun bun bouillon cubes.

Pernicious soup
in between sinking and floating
is soaking
the beans sink the bones
let the beans nap to be put to sleep
by the ocean let the salt sing
to the bones let the water sing to the beans
until they become tender
the ivory beans need to let
the bones tender themselves to the carrots
let the buttons lie gently in the ocean
very thick coins indeed.

A penny for your morning at the ocean?

This is a lesson
hidden in a saucepan
others will lie on their onion skins
so long as onions spin
in circles around garlic and vinegar
balsamic is their rosin
let this stick
the garlic will stick to the patient.

Julia Rose Lewis & Nathan Hyland Walker

A penny for your onion now?

A pat of butter is polite
as a cabbage patch kid living in the garden
cabbage is better rich and green.

If the sun is falling
and the cabbage is tired out, then night
adds this star very star little light caramel
to the ivory beans.

A penny for your rosemary?

If and only if you will
remember me to the spices tonight
and simmer very lovely the tomatoes stewed
and whisper to them very lowly until
velvet becomes the beans
and simmers very lovely the tomorrows stewed
and whispers very lowly
that velvet becomes the bones.

Beautiful soup so rich and green is it waiting
in a cauldron or a water trough in a field?

Remember to retrieve the bay leaves,
they are traveling in the bay
lee of windward, and always baling twine
will be unthreaded.

Whoever is a sap
for such dandelion greens would not stop
for the sponge of the evening
lively and sound
would in deed not sop up this lovely thoroughbred?

The Velvet Protocol

A penny for your racehorse?

Let the horse lie quietly for the night
her water bucket is full and her stall is left with half
a salt lick, a politeness
like butter is left to serve
with a nightmare with a crested neck and light head.

Julia Rose Lewis & Nathan Hyland Walker

Xanthan Gum
Xgeva

Row arrowroot,
oar after oar ranks cornstarch
row operations on the bone meat well met
is not the same as limits
to the activity of bone cells,
osteoclasts meant well themselves.

It is a gentle lie to let the thinking agent
see inside the boat
to give stickiness to limestone
to thicken the bones with pebbles.

Take calcium and tell a woman something new.

Merrily is as merry lies
shimmering against the corn sugar gum,
in this mirage,
gram negative bacteria grows.

Nearly a fancy string of sugars
if wrinkles scream
this grandmother screams for ice cream.

Life is oar after oar plus from more,
life is but a hierarchy of arms well meant.

The Navy Beans: Week 2

The Velvet Protocol

Premeds

Pepcid 40mg IVP
Solumedrol 15mg IVP

Julia Rose Lewis & Nathan Hyland Walker

Diet Pepsi
Pepcid

In the same lemon as gasoline,
soon gastrin
and the vagus nerve trigger release
of pepsinogen,
it digests itself today
now born pepsin sinning against the diner.

We hate it.

The mother of chaos is
the grandmother of gas and the road
from vast chasm void,
this obsidian is a glass and charcoal act
in between veins of history
I mean like a grandmother in her kitchen,
we take it.

We take another little piece of her volcanic rock
for relief if heartburn fizzes and dazes still.

People will tell you it leads towards cancer,
and I will laugh,
actually cackle like the witch
because coal or charcoal it is important to note
that gas came from chaos
to denote a principle if occult singing.

We respire it.

Sole Mediterranean Solumedrol

Instead of muddling with gin
never alone,
is sole the vehicle in the middle of dill,
lime, and capers,
see a dozen thin files like flatfish.

If sill and the sandal firmament will
allow the soul
to meddle with them garlic power, cumin, peppercorns,
and salt will become pavement.

Filling a midden of garlic and inexperienced onions,
unsalted, the butter becomes caper berries,
about to shallots,
obsolete leaps to cope as goats
says the nanny goat to the kid
remember generous is as generous does need.

Rough and fresh dill to garnish a foolish person
of the parsley family gives a delightful look,
silly in the sense of innocent luck,
musical chairs, dill leaves.

Eye of the grasshopper cheers!

Julia Rose Lewis & Nathan Hyland Walker
Antiemetics

Zofran 8mg IV

Saffron
Zofran

In the dominion nausea,
see saffron crocus sings autumn,
and the crows flower a darker lilac crocus sunlight.

Sun bright, satin knows what needs be done
and watches until it is the fragrant hay.

First style, I see saffron fresh,
I see one-hundred and fifty flowers dried is real life;
I wish in crimson,
I wish the stigma of witches in the distance,
I wish in triplet styles.

I have this wish for red maroon down to yellow dishes;
I wish for colors sargol, pushal, bunch, and konge,
with all this might.

Well make a window,
a week or two, and do as crimson dried and threads
sealed in dreams
and all the stigmas, all the wishes will come true,
will thread through saffron nurses.

Julia Rose Lewis & Nathan Hyland Walker
Chemotherapy

Navelbine 50mg

Navy Beans
Navelbine

If fee fie fight
then the beans must be life
night life means that magic comes
if foe fumes foam
when the magic comes over the bones
and the marrow would grow beans
and the marrow would grow white
and the marrow would do more for the artwork.

The rabbits lingering in the garden
over the vegans go save the narrow white beans
if the artifact will tell the beanstalk to tell
the rabbits all night,
stay this way,
stay these beans feasting on their greens.

The beans will be sure to measure the water,
maybe labradorite,
maybe pond scum comes to see through
the soaking of the beans.

They were bred for this magic
breaking apart the head of roast garlic caramel willing
and peeled with the windows full open fall
it will have been those ivory beans.

They were bread for reassuring the bones
the rabbits tell
the beans narrow clean and nothing marred
the body surface area before the monstrous normal
where vinegar red.

Julia Rose Lewis & Nathan Hyland Walker

The wine beside the bone narrows
the table salt only and never more than seven,
evergreens,
this is not yet the season to be full of leaves,
let them be,
let the legumes be beside themselves,
to let the magic smell the garlic,
not the bones,
magic beans are not born as haricot beans naturally.

These magic bones are born as easily as beans
the flavored marrow of the bones
is seasoning
in salt and wedding peppercorns
and garlic caramel
and the sweat of a princess
she is otherwise known
to blend into the dividends of being patient.

The green and grey and brown lend themselves to the
periwinkle plant indeed
these vinca alkaloids blend through out.

Spread true.

This dinner the bones will remember the vine
or beanstalk or magic vineyard turning into vinegar red.

Please remember the fritos and radishes to the rabbits.

Rest: Week 3

The Kitchen Sink without the Sponge: Week 4

Premeds

Pepcid 40mg IVP
Solumedrol 15mg IVP
Benedryl 25mg IVP
Demerol 12.5mg IV PRN x 1

Julia Rose Lewis & Nathan Hyland Walker

Diet Pepsi
Pepcid

In the same lemon as gasoline,
soon gastrin
and the vagus nerve trigger release
of pepsinogen,
it digests itself today
now born pepsin sinning against the diner.

We hate it.

The mother of chaos is
the grandmother of gas and the road
from vast chasm void,
this obsidian is a glass and charcoal act
in between veins of history
I mean like a grandmother in her kitchen,
we take it.

We take another little piece of her volcanic rock
for relief if heartburn fizzes and dazes still.

People will tell you it leads towards cancer,
and I will laugh,
actually cackle like the witch
because coal or charcoal it is important to note
that gas came from chaos
to denote a principle if occult singing.

We respire it.

Sole Mediterranean Solumedrol

Instead of muddling with gin
never alone,
is sole the vehicle in the middle of dill,
lime, and capers,
see a dozen thin files like flatfish.

If sill and the sandal firmament will
allow the soul
to meddle with them garlic power, cumin, peppercorns,
and salt will become pavement.

Filling a midden of garlic and inexperienced onions,
unsalted, the butter becomes caper berries,
about to shallots,
obsolete leaps to cope as goats
says the nanny goat to the kid
remember generous is as generous does need.

Rough and fresh dill to garnish a foolish person
of the parsley family gives a delightful look,
silly in the sense of innocent luck,
musical chairs, dill leaves.

Eye of the grasshopper cheers!

Julia Rose Lewis & Nathan Hyland Walker

Beignets
Benedryl

In begetting,
use sugar reverse beer,
if feeding let alone ten minutes and it will foam.

A little feral besting the eggs, salt,
evaporated milk, and then mix the two measures.

Stir half the flour for the shortening
for the stirring into this meaning before others.

Lightening needs.

Transfer to fat and bowl with towel,
and do not disturb for two hours or here.

From the bed of the problem, roll out tired bodies,
they are fried in the deep sense of tried.

This feral lift off will leave inside the hollow lies
as the beignets are finished
in kind to wooden boats.

After dry draining they are given to satin navigation.

The sugar coat will let the sailboat into the wind
and begging the vigor of history I mean.

Antiemetics

Ativan 0.5mg IV PRN
Zofran 8mg IV

Julia Rose Lewis & Nathan Hyland Walker
Saffron
Zofran

In the dominion nausea,
see saffron crocus sings autumn,
and the crows flower a darker lilac crocus sunlight.

Sun bright, satin knows what needs be done
and watches until it is the fragrant hay.

First style, I see saffron fresh,
I see one-hundred and fifty flowers dried is real life;
I wish in crimson,
I wish the stigma of witches in the distance,
I wish in triplet styles.

I have this wish for red maroon down to yellow dishes;
I wish for colors sargol, pushal, bunch, and konge,
with all this might.

Well make a window,
a week or two, and do as crimson dried and threads
sealed in dreams
and all the stigmas, all the wishes will come true,
will thread through saffron nurses.

Chemotherapy

Herceptin 825mg IV
Perjeta 420mg IV
Navelbine 50mg IV

Julia Rose Lewis & Nathan Hyland Walker

Hare, Ceps, and Wine Herceptin

The leading hare,
in quarters read dimerization
here cut into seven or eight and brined daytime.

Perception stirs at flour, pepper,
and further salt tossing the hare to coat
in the earthenware oven,
clarified butter is fine to warm two pats to brown
the hare in parts to braise its coat.

Raise the hare,
in the season of natural utterance running
fast to praise her interception.

One large carrot sliced into the earthenware,
add two large onions diced, add the third butter
and sauté until golden onions.

Here print the thyme from the leavings
of five or six sprigs and stir into the earthenware
and stir in five cloves of garlic.

Now wine in order, the hare burgundy to return,
to the earth then weathering
until thinking for thirty minutes more
and more before removing to let simmer itself thick.

On the inception of porcini mushrooms,
from stake and pores,
in a separate pan, it is fine to clarify butter to hear
the penny buns to understand
to entirely take the ceps, stalk, and caps inside.

The Velvet Protocol

Perceive the history of the stone noble,
its nitrogen exchange in the white and pine forest
it is known as squirrels bread.

Once upon a time the boulder in the woodland
and now wine in butter reception,
this garnish was always to finish with parsley as the
mutual tomorrow.

Julia Rose Lewis & Nathan Hyland Walker

Bruschetta
Perjeta

Bruschetta is bread and
red and bread
and red tomatoes and yellow tomorrows and orange
tomatoes
and green tomorrows
and purple tomatoes looming
in the middle of the Thursday
and through this day which is old.

The bread should be day old
before toasting,
before rubbing with roast garlic,
do not roast the tomatoes
for they are summoning her
to balsamic, to salt, to pepper, tomorrow.

Now throw the tomato
dice into the bowl with seeds up, with skins up, face up
to
macerate to make soft or made soft or soaked,
to soften in olive from oil
from olive for extra virgin olive oil… the future of oil is
leaving here.

So seeds up, sixes up
to fill the bread,
let the tomatoes fall softly
only onto the bread yet,
bruschetta is simple is still experimental, appetizer a part
of a whole protocol, please see
the velvet protocol.

Navy Bean Soup
Navelbine

What is up?
Soup!
Soup?
It is navy bean soup day
it is Thursday
it is one Thursday in four through the day
though the day
today is the day to take the kitchen sink inside the vein
think navy bean soup days
think kitchen sink days
think about putting everything into a prayer into a vein.

Put the navy beans into the soup pot
pour them over with eight cups of water to cover
separate the beans from the air
put the beans under water at a low simmer
simmer slowly
let the beans lie gently in the sea until
tender with stirring into the carrots stirring into the
beans
the syringe measures a mature carrot
a farmed carrot is the measure of this syringe needed to
brighten the sea
tenderly brighten the sea.

Onion in onion in garlic is given
in between the venous intravenous
is the given injection a gift with a push of the thumbs
is it possible to feel the pushing in the veins
like it is possible to taste the saline flushing through the
day
the saline flush is how we finish the day

Julia Rose Lewis & Nathan Hyland Walker

savor we the dessert
caramel lies the onion in vinegar
balsamic vinegar lies low on the heat until sweet.

In order to continue to sauté
continue to add liquid
as required add one cup cabbage
and as needed add one cup of celery leaves
these leaves with tender inner stalks chopped quite fine
and as demanded add five garlic cloves minced.

Then wait until when the mixture has cooked down
inside the pan
when the cabbage has cooked the mixture down
when the celery is long past translucent
when the flavor of the garlic is in the liquid
then add to the navy beans to simmer star very star
slowly
so remember the thyme and the tomato sauce and the
other assorted spices
simmer very lovely
simmer the very lowly until velvet becomes the beans.

Remember in time to remove the bay leaves
bay lee of windward
baling twine
let the horse lie quietly for the night
her water bucket is full and her stall is left with one-half
a salt lick
like butter left to serve with a nightmare with a crested
neck and light head.

The Navy Beans: Week 5

Premeds

Pepcid 40mg IVP
Solumedrol 15mg IVP

Julia Rose Lewis & Nathan Hyland Walker

Diet Pepsi
Pepcid

In the same lemon as gasoline,
soon gastrin
and the vagus nerve trigger release
of pepsinogen,
it digests itself today
now born pepsin sinning against the diner.

We hate it.

The mother of chaos is
the grandmother of gas and the road
from vast chasm void,
this obsidian is a glass and charcoal act
in between veins of history
I mean like a grandmother in her kitchen,
we take it.

We take another little piece of her volcanic rock
for relief if heartburn fizzes and dazes still.

People will tell you it leads towards cancer,
and I will laugh,
actually cackle like the witch
because coal or charcoal it is important to note
that gas came from chaos
to denote a principle if occult singing.

We respire it.

Sole Mediterranean Solumedrol

Instead of muddling with gin
never alone,
is sole the vehicle in the middle of dill,
lime, and capers,
see a dozen thin files like flatfish.

If sill and the sandal firmament will
allow the soul
to meddle with them garlic power, cumin, peppercorns,
and salt will become pavement.

Filling a midden of garlic and inexperienced onions,
unsalted, the butter becomes caper berries,
about to shallots,
obsolete leaps to cope as goats
says the nanny goat to the kid
remember generous is as generous does need.

Rough and fresh dill to garnish a foolish person
of the parsley family gives a delightful look,
silly in the sense of innocent luck,
musical chairs, dill leaves.

Eye of the grasshopper cheers!

Julia Rose Lewis & Nathan Hyland Walker
Antiemetics

Zofran 8mg IV

Saffron
Zofran

In the dominion nausea,
see saffron crocus sings autumn,
and the crows flower a darker lilac crocus sunlight.

Sun bright, satin knows what needs be done
and watches until it is the fragrant hay.

First style, I see saffron fresh,
I see one-hundred and fifty flowers dried is real life;
I wish in crimson,
I wish the stigma of witches in the distance,
I wish in triplet styles.

I have this wish for red maroon down to yellow dishes;
I wish for colors sargol, pushal, bunch, and konge,
with all this might.

Well make a window,
a week or two, and do as crimson dried and threads
sealed in dreams
and all the stigmas, all the wishes will come true,
will thread through saffron nurses.

Julia Rose Lewis & Nathan Hyland Walker

Chemotherapy

Navelbine 50mg IV

Navy Beans
Navelbine

If fee fie fight
then the beans must be life
night life means that magic comes
if foe fumes foam
when the magic comes over the bones
and the marrow would grow beans
and the marrow would grow white
and the marrow would do more for the artwork.

The rabbits lingering in the garden
over the vegans go save the narrow white beans
if the artifact will tell the beanstalk to tell
the rabbits all night,
stay this way,
stay these beans feasting on their greens.

The beans will be sure to measure the water,
maybe labradorite,
maybe pond scum comes to see through
the soaking of the beans.

They were bred for this magic
breaking apart the head of roast garlic caramel willing
and peeled with the windows full open fall
it will have been those ivory beans.

They were bread for reassuring the bones
the rabbits tell
the beans narrow clean and nothing marred
the body surface area before the monstrous normal
where vinegar red.

Julia Rose Lewis & Nathan Hyland Walker

The wine beside the bone narrows
the table salt only and never more than seven,
evergreens,
this is not yet the season to be full of leaves,
let them be,
let the legumes be beside themselves,
to let the magic smell the garlic,
not the bones,
magic beans are not born as haricot beans naturally.

These magic bones are born as easily as beans
the flavored marrow of the bones
is seasoning
in salt and wedding peppercorns
and garlic caramel
and the sweat of a princess
she is otherwise known
to blend into the dividends of being patient.

The green and grey and brown lend themselves to the
periwinkle plant indeed
these vinca alkaloids blend true.

Spread true.

This dinner, the bones will remember the vine or beanstalk or
magic vineyard turning into vinegar red.

Please remember the fritos and radishes to the rabbits.

Rest: Week 6

The End of the Beginning

It is important to note that the dose of Navelbine can be increased if the patient's disease begins to progress on the velvet protocol.

Into night the disease progresses. Enter the nightmare, there are three methods for determining chemo dose, fixed dosing, weight-based dosing, and body surface area dosing. The velvet protocol calls for fixed dosing for Perjeta, weight-based dosing of Herceptin, and body surface area dosing for Navelbine. Body surface area is calculated with one of many simple formulae based on the height and weight of the patient. Scientists thought that body surface area correlated well to blood volume and therefore, to kidney and liver function. Courtesy of nature that has been proven problematic in certain patient types. Anyone who has ever witnessed a miniature horse mare urinate will understand.

The Velvet Protocol Artifacts

Retirement and the White Rabbit

On having your red velvet cake and having your red wine as well. It will be sour in the stead of bitter. The velvet protocol lends a quality of life to the patient terminal which is not unlike a red velvet cake. Life starts as a recipe for an experience like the cake on the back of the Hershey's cocoa powder box, illness will change the receipt, and therefore, change the experience of living with illness. The evolution of stories stories of evolution will lead to the lifespan falling between that of wild and domestic rabbits.

Julia Rose Lewis & Nathan Hyland Walker

Beginning of the End

two cups granulated sugar
two and one-quarter cups all purpose flour
one quarter cup dutch processed cocoa
one and a half teaspoons baking soda
one and a half teaspoons baking powder
one teaspoon salt
three eggs
one cup pinot noir
one half cup vegetable oil
two teaspoons vanilla extract
insult to use one cup boiling pinot noir?

All the Velvet

Is it insulting to my sister to use the wine from the vineyard she is running? Once upon a time, my sister mocked me for using so much red food coloring for the birthday cake in the stead of beets. Red dark color following in the sense workmanship from free will from art to make. Heat oven to three-hundred and fifty degrees. Line with parchment a pair of nine inch round baking pans. Combine the dry ingredients in a standing mixer, and combine again with eggs, wine, oil, and vanilla absolutely, thoroughly, the story of a girl.

Julia Rose Lewis & Nathan Hyland Walker
Trinity River Velvet

Free will is not a stripper name. The red and yellow helmet, velvet brown is using art the past participle of the verb to make the heirloom money. Stir in boiling wine, be sure to stir through and through the batter will be thin. Bake until the wooden pick inserted into the cake comes out without cake. Let the cake become quite cool and dust with powdered sugar to taste. It will yield the liver chestnut, the red velvet of horses. Receipt of the pirate, the murderous pirate undeserving of a name, the nickname pie and all the little irrational girls.

Author Bios

Julia Rose Lewis is the author of three poetry collections: *Phenomenology of the Feral* (KFS), *High Erratic Ecology* (KFS), and *The Hen Wife* (Contraband). She and James Miller co-authored *Strays* (HVTN). She has published seven pamphlets, the most recent of which is *Holding Patterns* with Paul Hawkins (Beir Bua Press).

Nathan Hyland Walker graduated from The Culinary Institute of America in 2012. He has worked in kitchens including The Fog Island Cafe, The Fog Island Grille, Vescio's, Pizza Boys, and The Tap Room. He now works as head chef for the residents of a memory care facility in New York.

www.ingramcontent.com/pod-product-compliance
Lightning Source LLC
Chambersburg PA
CBHW010854090426

42736CB00020B/3455